zendoodle coloring
COLOR-by-NUMBER

Stained Glass

zendoodle coloring
COLOR-by-NUMBER

Stained Glass

Dazzling Art to Color and Display

illustrations by

Deborah Muller

ST. MARTIN'S GRIFFIN

NEW YORK

www.stmartins.com

ISBN 978-1-250-14919-0 (trade paperback)

Our books may be purchased in bulk for promotional, educational, or business use.
Please contact your local bookseller or the Macmillan Corporate and Premium
Sales Department at 1-800-221-7945, extension 5442, or by e-mail
at MacmillanSpecialMarkets@macmillan.com.

First Edition: November 2017

10 9 8 7 6 5 4 3 2 1

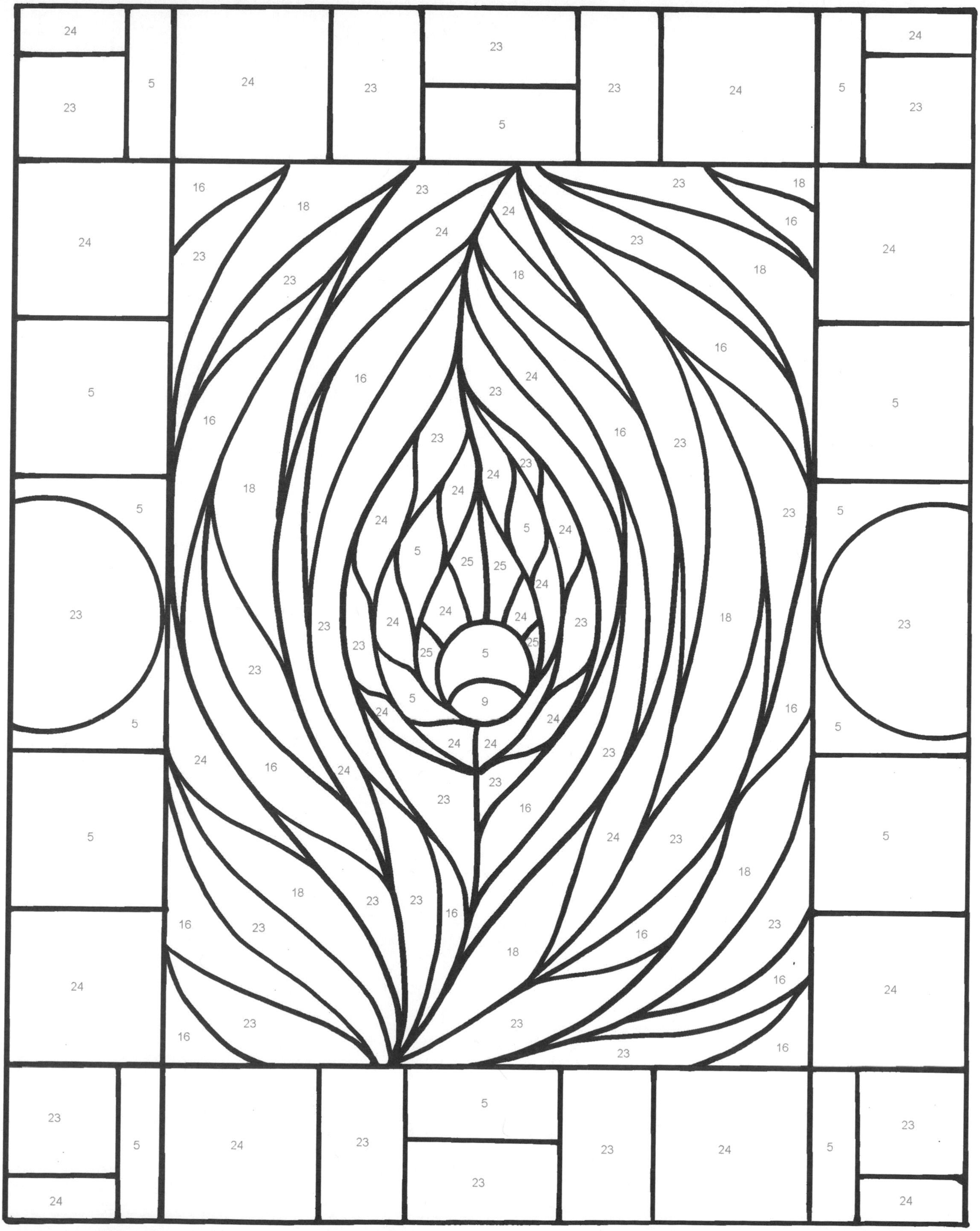

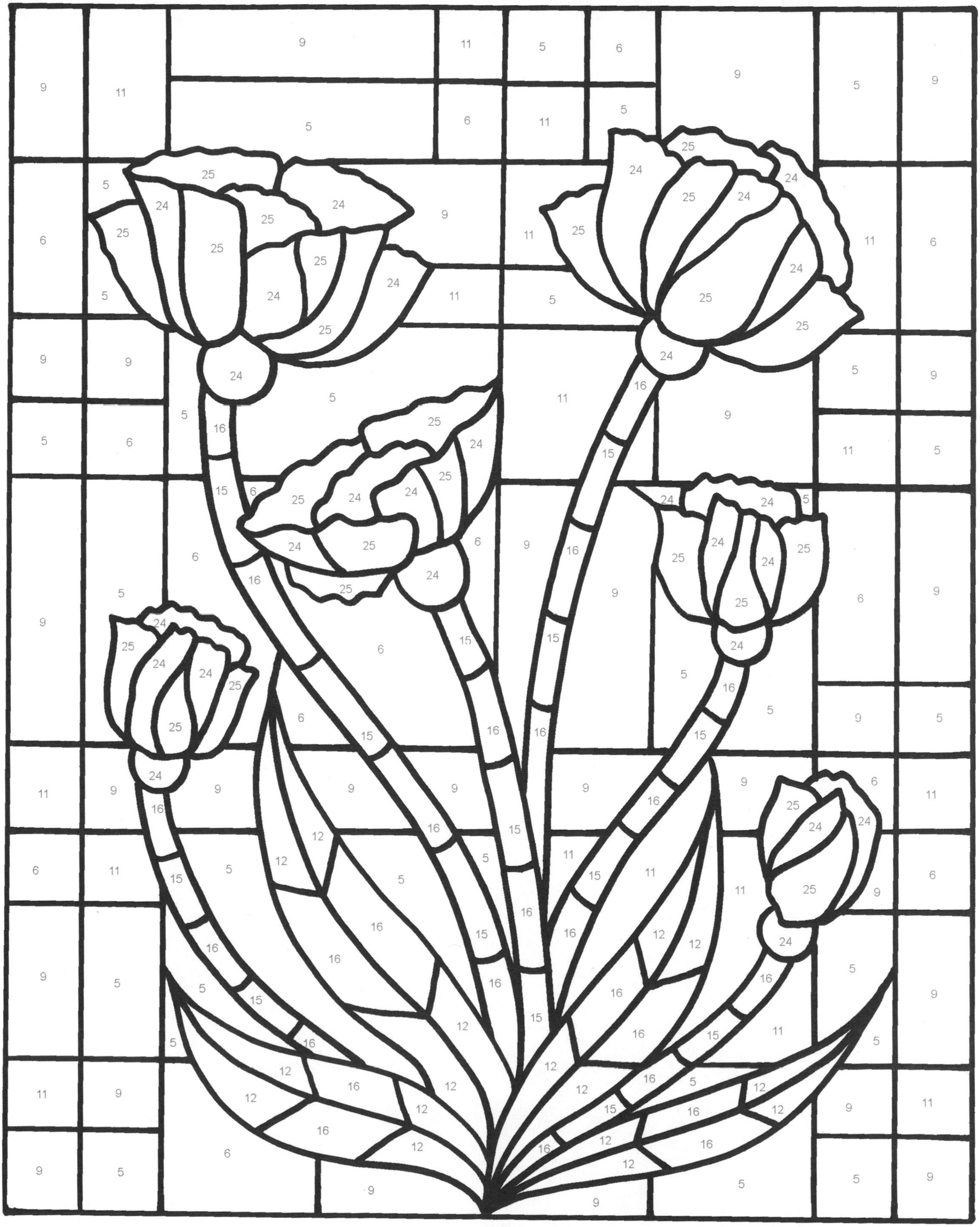

Other great books in the series

zendoodle
color-by-number series

Spring Awakening

Sea Life

Playful Pets

Other great books in the

zendoodle coloring series

Celestial Wonders

Loving Expressions

Baby Animals

Birds & Butterflies

Magical Mermaid Kitties

Playful Puppies

Hopeful Inspirations

and many more!